D1709245

DANGEROUS ADVENTURES

Ballooning Adventures

by Glen and Karen Bledsoe

Consultant:
Ruth P. Ludwig
Editor, *Ballooning: The Journal of the
Balloon Federation of America*

CAPSTONE BOOKS
an imprint of Capstone Press
Mankato, Minnesota

Capstone Books are published by Capstone Press
151 Good Counsel Drive, P.O. Box 669, Mankato, Minnesota 56002
http://www.capstone-press.com

Library of Congress Cataloging-in-Publication Data
Bledsoe, Glen.
    Ballooning adventures/by Glen and Karen Bledsoe.
    p. cm.—(Dangerous adventures)
    Includes bibliographical references (p. 45) and index.
    Summary: Describes the different types of balloons, the history and dangers of
ballooning, and some aeronauts' adventures.
    ISBN 0-7368-0574-5
    1. Ballooning—Juvenile literature. [1. Ballooning.] I. Bledsoe, Karen E. II. Title.
III. Series.
GV762 . B54 2001
797.5'1—dc21   00-024997

Editorial Credits
Carrie A. Braulick, editor; Heather Kindseth, cover designer and illustrator;
    Linda Clavel, illustrator; Katy Kudela and Jodi Theisen, photo researchers

Photo Credits
Al Satterwhite/FPG International LLC, 8; FPG International LLC, 21
Archive Photos, 10, 12, 22, 25
Gerard Fritz/Photo Agora, 40
Index Stock Imagery, cover, 4, 17, 34
John Ninomiya, 42
Northwind Picture Archives, 14, 18
TRANS PAC, 28, 31, 33
Visuals Unlimited/D. Clayton, 7
Voscar The Maine Photographer, 26

1 2 3 4 5 6 06 05 04 03 02 01

Thank you to John Ninomiya for his assistance in preparing this book.

Table of Contents

Chapter 1 Ballooning 5

Chapter 2 Famous Firsts 15

Chapter 3 Across the Atlantic and
North America 23

Chapter 4 Across the Pacific 29

Chapter 5 Around the World 35

Chapter 6 The Future of Ballooning 41

Features

Breitling Orbiter 3 Route 36

Timeline 38

Words to Know 44

To Learn More 45

Useful Addresses 46

Internet Sites 47

Index 48

Chapter 1

Ballooning

On March 1, 1999, Bertrand Piccard and Brian Jones launched their balloon in Switzerland. They planned to travel around the world in their balloon without stopping. No one had ever completed this journey. Piccard and Jones' balloon was called *Breitling Orbiter 3*.

The pilots encountered problems during the journey. The wind speed sometimes decreased. Their fuel supply ran low. Piccard and Jones were worried that they would need to end their flight. But on March 20, 1999, Piccard and Jones landed *Breitling Orbiter 3* in Egypt. They had accomplished their goal of traveling around the world.

Balloon pilots ride in gondolas. These baskets or enclosed cabins hang underneath a balloon's

Bertrand Piccard was one of the pilots who traveled in *Breitling Orbiter 3*.

envelope. The envelope is the large bag that holds the hot air or gas that makes a balloon rise. A balloon's envelope is made of fabric or plastic. Fabric envelopes usually are coated with urethane. This material prevents the air or gas from leaking out of the envelope.

Many pilots fly balloons for sport. Communities may hold balloon races. Balloon pilots may take passengers up in balloons for rides. Some pilots enjoy greater challenges. These pilots may fly across oceans or try to break ballooning records.

Types of Balloons

Three main types of balloons exist. The elements inside all of these balloons are lighter than air. These elements make the balloons rise.

Two brothers from France named Joseph Michel and Jacques Étienne Montgolfier invented hot-air balloons. These balloons also are called Montgolfier balloons. The air inside these balloons is heated to become warmer and lighter than the outside air. The warm air causes the balloons to rise.

Hot-air balloon pilots use burners to heat the air in their balloons.

Hot-air balloons have burners located between the balloon's envelope and the gondola. The burners keep the air inside the balloon heated. Pilots increase and decrease the air's temperature in hot-air balloons to make the balloons rise and sink. They turn on the burner to make the air's temperature increase. They leave the burner off when they want the air's temperature to decrease.

Gas balloon pilots drop ballast to make their balloons rise.

Jacques Charles invented gas balloons. These balloons also are called Charlière balloons. Early gas balloons contained hydrogen gas. Hydrogen is lighter than air. But static electricity can cause hydrogen to start on fire. Fires can happen when the balloon rubs against itself or another type of material. A fire can cause the balloon to crash.

Today's hydrogen balloons are coated with rubber. The coating helps prevent static electricity. European pilots often fly hydrogen balloons. But many pilots fly gas balloons filled with helium. This gas also is lighter than air. But it does not catch fire like hydrogen does.

Pilots fly gas balloons differently from hot-air balloons. Gas balloon pilots put bags of sand or other heavy material into their gondolas. This material is called ballast. The pilots drop ballast to make the balloons rise. Gas balloon pilots release gas from their balloons to make them sink. They pull a rope that runs from the envelope to the gondola to release the gas. The gas then flows through a small valve in the top of the envelope. A valve is a movable part that controls the flow of air or gas through a tube.

The sun's heat causes balloons to expand. Gas balloons will rip if they inflate too much. Some gas balloon pilots avoid this danger by coating their balloons' envelopes with Mylar. This thin, strong material reflects the sun's rays and prevents the balloons from expanding.

Some balloons combine gas and heat. These balloons are called Rozier balloons. They are named after the first balloon pilot. His name was Pilâtre de Rozier. Rozier balloons have a container filled with hot air above their gondolas. A container of gas is located above the hot air. Pilots heat the air with a burner. The air then heats the gas. The hot gas gives Rozier balloons more lift than other balloons. Lift is the force that pulls balloons up into the air.

Long-Distance Balloons
Some balloon pilots plan to travel long distances. They may want to fly across oceans or around the world. These pilots may fly in any one of the three balloon types. But these balloons must be very large.

Balloon sizes are measured by the amount of air they hold. Hot-air balloons are measured in cubic feet. Standard hot-air balloons hold 77,000 to 100,000 cubic feet (2,179 to 2,830 cubic meters) of air. Gas balloons are measured in cubic meters. Standard gas balloons usually hold about 1,000 cubic meters (35,315 cubic feet) of gas. Long-distance balloons may be about

The large size of long-distance balloons allows them to carry more weight than smaller balloons.

Gondolas in long-distance balloons often have communication equipment.

three times larger than standard balloons. Small balloons cannot carry the weight of the ballast, fuel, and other supplies necessary for long-distance flights.

Supplies and Equipment

Large, long-distance balloons can carry the weight of supplies necessary for long journeys. They carry extra fuel and ballast. They also must carry enough food and water for the entire flight. Some gondolas in long-distance balloons have a small stove. Long-distance gondolas usually have narrow cots for sleeping.

Long-distance balloons also may carry communication equipment. They may have radios. Pilots can use the radios to talk to people on the ground. Long-distance gondolas also may have on-board computers. Pilots can connect these computers to the Internet. They then can communicate with others through their computers.

Gondolas

Long-distance balloons usually have enclosed gondolas. These gondolas help protect the pilots and equipment from bad weather conditions. Enclosed gondolas also help protect pilots from cold temperatures at high altitudes.

Pilots who fly long distances may use pressurized gondolas. Pressurized gondolas allow people to breathe normally when balloons fly at high altitudes. Air at these heights contains little oxygen for people to breathe. Pressurized gondolas have tanks that supply oxygen to the pilots. Pilots who use unpressurized gondolas may need to use masks to breathe oxygen from tanks at high altitudes.

Chapter 2

Famous Firsts

Ballooning began in the late 1700s. Joseph Michel and Jacques Étienne Montgolfier owned a paper factory. The brothers noticed that smoke would rise from a burning fire. They thought that smoke might also lift balloons. In 1782, they experimented with paper bags. They floated these bags over their kitchen fire. They soon made balloons out of paper and linen to float over their fire.

The two brothers believed thick smoke created better lift. At first, they burned old shoes, rotten meat, rags soaked in alcohol, and wet straw. But soon they discovered it was hot air that actually lifted balloons.

Many people watched the first hot-air balloon flights in 1783.

The First Balloon Flights

No one was sure how safe it was to fly in a hot-air balloon. On September 19, 1783, the Montgolfier brothers sent a sheep, rooster, and duck on the first balloon ride. The animals were in a tethered balloon. These balloons are attached to the ground by ropes. The brothers named the balloon *Revellion II*. The animals landed safely.

People soon flew in hot-air balloons. On October 15, 1783, Pilâtre de Rozier flew in a tethered balloon. Rozier landed safely. On November 21, 1783, Rozier and Marquis François Laurent d'Arlandes became the first people to fly in an untethered balloon. They flew about 27 miles (43 kilometers).

Jacques Charles launched the first hydrogen gas balloon on August 27, 1783. The balloon flew over people in a small French village called Gonesse. These people had never seen a balloon before. They did not understand what it was. They believed it was a monster. The

Pilots began to fly gas balloons in December 1783.

villagers attacked the balloon with knives and pitchforks when it landed. No one was hurt because the balloon did not carry a pilot.

On December 1, 1783, Jacques Charles and Noël Robert became the first pilots of a gas balloon. They flew for about 2 hours and traveled nearly 30 miles (48 kilometers).

A Ballooning Accident

Hot-air balloons can travel only short distances if they cool down. Early pilots learned to heat the air with a fire in a metal basket. Hot-air balloons then could travel longer distances. Hydrogen balloons could travel even farther than hot-air balloons because they did not need to carry fuel.

Some pilots wanted to design balloons that would travel even farther. Rozier experimented with balloons. He decided to mix hydrogen and hot air in a balloon. He believed the mixture would allow the balloon to stay in the air longer. On June 15, 1785, Rozier and Pierre Romain flew a balloon that used hydrogen and hot air. Both pilots died when the balloon started on fire.

Ballooning's Popularity Grows

Many people became interested in flying balloons. Some of these people wanted to take photographs from the air in balloons. Gaspand-Félix Tournachon was the world's first aerial photographer. People often called him "Nadar." Tournachon took pictures during the 1860s. His balloon was called

Ballooning remained popular throughout the 1800s.

Le Géant. This means "The Giant." Tournachon's first aerial photographs were of the city of Paris.

Women also were interested in flying balloons. In 1784, Elisabeth Thible became the first woman to fly in a balloon. Thible was a French opera singer. She asked a friend to take her on a balloon ride. In 1798, Jeanne Labrosse became the first woman to fly a balloon alone.

Balloons in War

Some people realized balloons could be used for more than just recreation. The French Revolution (1787–1799) began when French citizens overthrew the government. The war later involved countries such as the Netherlands and Austria. In June 1794, French soldiers used a tethered gas balloon to spy on their enemies. Two soldiers were in the balloon's gondola. One soldier used a telescope to watch the enemy soldiers. The other soldier took notes.

Soldiers also used balloons in the U.S. Civil War (1861–1865) between Northern states and Southern states. They ran wire telegraph lines from the balloons to the ground. The pilots

Military forces around the world continued to use balloons for war purposes during the early 1900s.

searched for enemy troops. They then sent messages across the telegraph lines to soldiers on the ground. These messages helped the ground soldiers keep track of enemy movements.

Many countries used balloons during later wars. For example, military forces often used balloons during World War I (1914–1918) and World War II (1939–1945).

Chapter 3

Across the Atlantic and North America

Pilots who fly balloons long distances face many challenges and dangers. Ice sometimes forms on balloons at high altitudes. The weight of the ice can cause balloons to sink. Strong winds during storms may blow balloons off course. Leaders of some countries may not allow pilots to fly over their territory.

Early pilots tried to fly the longest distances possible. Several pilots tried to cross the Atlantic Ocean to make the first transoceanic flight. Other balloon pilots tried to cross a continent to make the first transcontinental flight.

Double Eagle II was the first balloon to travel across the Atlantic Ocean.

Double Eagle II

In 1978, Maxie Anderson, Larry Newman, and Ben Abruzzo made the first transoceanic flight. They flew across the Atlantic Ocean in a gas balloon called *Double Eagle II*. They traveled a distance of about 3,000 miles (4,800 kilometers).

The pilots prepared for their journey. The gondola was partly enclosed. It had a heater. But the pilots still could become cold. The crew dressed in layers of wool clothing to stay warm. Abruzzo wore electric socks. These socks produced heat. His feet had been painfully frostbitten on an earlier balloon flight. This condition occurs when cold temperatures freeze skin. The pilots brought masks and oxygen tanks with them. This allowed them to breathe easily at high altitudes.

Double Eagle II launched from Presque Isle, Maine, on August 11, 1978. On the fourth night, ice built up on the balloon. The weight of the ice caused the balloon to sink. But the ice melted when the sun came up and the balloon rose again.

On August 16, *Double Eagle II* began to drop. It fell from about 25,000 feet (7,620 meters) to

Maxie Anderson, Ben Abruzzo, and Larry Newman were the pilots of *Double Eagle II*.

4,000 feet (1,219 meters). The crew slowly let out ballast until the balloon began to rise again.

On August 17, *Double Eagle II* landed in Miserey, France. The balloon had flown for 137 hours and 6 minutes. The people in France were excited about the pilots' successful trip. Many of them wanted a souvenir. They took the crew's maps and logs. Some people even tried to chew the balloon apart to take a piece home.

Joe Kittinger launched *Rosie O' Grady* from Caribou, Maine.

Kitty Hawk

In 1980, Maxie Anderson and his son Kristian made the first transcontinental flight in a gas balloon called *Kitty Hawk*. The pilots launched the balloon in Fort Baker, California.

The pilots had problems during their flight. Winds blew them off course. Temperatures sometimes were so cold that their drinking water froze. Maxie got sick. But the Andersons did not stop. They landed in a tree in Quebec, Canada. The trip lasted four days. The Andersons had covered about 2,400 miles (4,000 kilometers).

Other Flights

Double Eagle II was the first gas balloon to cross the Atlantic Ocean. But Per Lindstrand and Richard Branson wanted to make the same trip in a hot-air balloon. On July 4, 1987, they flew across the Atlantic Ocean in a hot-air balloon called *Virgin Atlantic Flyer*. The trip took about 31 hours. This was longer than anyone had ever flown in a hot-air balloon.

Joe Kittinger was the first person to fly solo across the Atlantic Ocean. His gas balloon was named *Rosie O' Grady*. On September 14, 1984, Kittinger began his flight in Caribou, Maine. He landed in Savona, Italy, four days later.

Chapter 4

Across the Pacific

Many early balloon pilots tried to cross the Atlantic Ocean. But few tried to fly across the Pacific Ocean. The Pacific Ocean is much wider than the Atlantic Ocean.

The first balloons to successfully cross the Pacific Ocean carried bombs instead of pilots. During World War II, Japan's military tried to bomb the northwestern coast of the United States. The Japanese military attached bombs to paper balloons. They planned that the wind would carry the balloons to the United States. The bombs would then explode and start large forest fires. But the forests on the coast were too wet. The bombs caused little damage.

Double Eagle V was the first piloted balloon to fly across the Pacific Ocean.

Double Eagle V

Double Eagle V was the first piloted balloon to successfully cross the Pacific Ocean. The pilots were Rocky Aoki, Ron Clark, Larry Newman, and Ben Abruzzo.

Double Eagle V was a gas balloon. Its envelope was painted silver to reflect the sun's rays. The gondola was not pressurized. The crew used masks and tanks to breathe oxygen at high altitudes. A heater kept the gondola warm.

The balloon launched from Nagashima, Japan, on the morning of November 10, 1981. Later that morning, ice built up on the balloon and caused it to sink. But the ice melted in the afternoon. The balloon rose as the sun warmed it. A storm soon forced the balloon down again. But the pilots were able to continue their flight.

Near California's coast, ice built up on the balloon again. The weight of the ice was about 3 tons (2.7 metric tons). The ice nearly forced the balloon down into the ocean. But it melted and fell off in large chunks.

Ben Abruzzo was one of *Double Eagle V's* pilots.

Another storm then caused problems for the pilots. The crew almost landed in the northern California town of Willits. But the pilots were afraid they would land on top of houses. The crew threw out ballast to make the balloon rise. They then landed near Covelo, California, on November 12, 1981. This town is about 30 miles (48 kilometers) south of Willets. The flight lasted 84 hours and 31 minutes. It covered about 5,000 miles (8,000 kilometers).

Other Pacific Flights

In 1991, pilots Richard Branson and Per Lindstrand made the first hot-air balloon flight across the Pacific Ocean. Their large balloon was named *Pacific Flyer*. It held 2.6 million cubic feet (73,580 cubic meters) of air.

Branson and Lindstrand launched *Pacific Flyer* from Japan on January 15, 1991. The balloon landed in northern Canada on January 17. It traveled about 6,700 miles (10,800 kilometers). The journey set a new record for the longest distance ever traveled by a balloon.

In 1995, Steve Fossett completed the first solo balloon flight across the Pacific Ocean. He launched the Rozier balloon *Solo Challenger* from Seoul, Korea, on February 14. He landed in Mendham, Saskatchewan, Canada, on February 17. Fossett traveled about 5,400 miles (8,700 kilometers).

Double Eagle V traveled about 5,000 miles (8,000 kilometers).

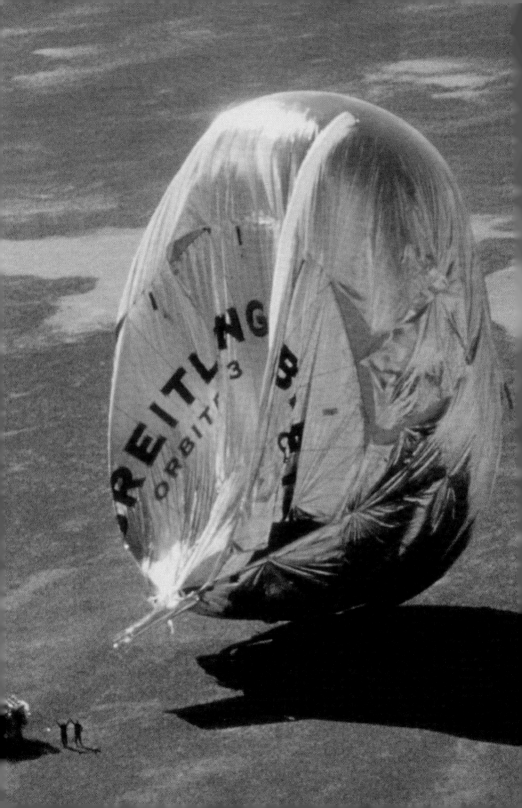

Chapter 5

Around the World

Successful flights across the Atlantic and Pacific Oceans were great accomplishments. But many pilots wanted to make a non-stop flight around the world.

The Race to be First

The first attempts to make a non-stop flight around the world were made in 1981 and 1982. Maxie Anderson and Don Ida flew in a balloon called *Jules Verne* during these flights. Helium leaks in the balloon's envelope forced the pilots to land during these attempts.

Several pilots made around-the-world attempts in the 1990s. Many of the flights lasted only one or two days. Bad weather forced some of the balloons down. Others had equipment problems.

Breitling Orbiter 3 landed in Egypt on March 21, 1999.

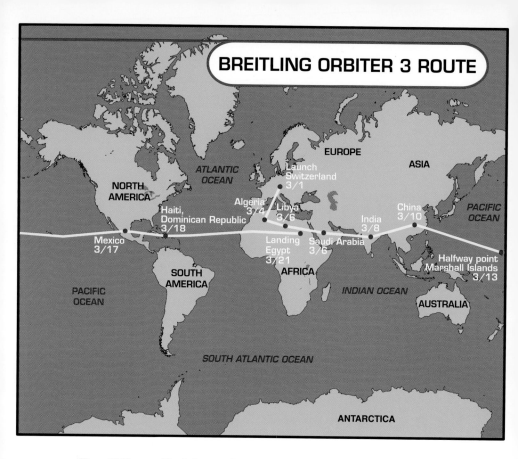

BREITLING ORBITER 3 ROUTE

EUROPE

ASIA

ATLANTIC
OCEAN

Launch
Switzerland
3/1

NORTH
AMERICA

Algeria
3/4

Libya
3/6

China
3/10

PACIFIC
OCEAN

Haiti,
Dominican Republic
3/18

India
3/8

Mexico
3/17

Landing
Egypt
3/21

Saudi Arabia
3/6

Halfway point
Marshall Islands
3/13

SOUTH
AMERICA

AFRICA

PACIFIC
OCEAN

INDIAN OCEAN

AUSTRALIA

SOUTH ATLANTIC OCEAN

ANTARCTICA

Breitling Orbiter 3

In 1999, pilots Bertrand Piccard and Brian
Jones prepared for an around-the-world flight.
On March 1, Piccard and Jones launched
Breitling Orbiter 3 from Switzerland. At first,
the Rozier balloon made good progress. The
balloon crossed China in 15 hours. It next
traveled over the Pacific Ocean. It crossed the
ocean in about six days. The jet stream carried

the balloon 115 miles (185 kilometers) per hour. This strong wind usually travels west to east at high altitudes.

Piccard and Jones later encountered problems. They were blown off course and lost the jet stream while they flew over Mexico. Piccard and Jones were afraid the flight would have to end. But people on the ground checked weather patterns for the pilots. They helped Piccard and Jones find the jet stream again.

On March 18, Piccard and Jones began their journey across the Atlantic Ocean. They traveled 105 miles (169 kilometers) per hour and crossed the ocean in four days. On March 20, they saw Africa's coastline. It took the team only one day to cross northern Africa.

On March 20, the pilots completed their around-the-world flight. Piccard and Jones landed the balloon at Mut, Egypt, on March 21, 1999. Their journey lasted 19 days, 21 hours, and 47 minutes. They traveled 25,361 miles (40,813 kilometers).

BALLOONING

1700s

1800s

JUNE 4, 1783
Joseph Michel and Jacques Étienne Montgolfier send up a balloon made of paper and linen.

NOVEMBER 21, 1783
François Laurent d' Arlandes and Pilâtre de Rozier become the first people to fly in an untethered balloon.

DECEMBER 1, 1783
Nöel Robert and Jacques Charles become the first pilots of a gas balloon.

JUNE 4, 1784
Elisabeth Thible becomes the first woman to travel in a balloon.

JUNE 23, 1784
Thirteen-year-old Edward Warren is the first U.S. citizen to go up in a tethered balloon.

JANUARY 9, 1793
Jean Pierre François Blanchard makes the first untethered flight in the United States.

JUNE 2, 1794
Balloons are first used in war. The French send up a balloon with two soldiers to spy on enemy forces during the French Revolution.

1798
Jeanne Labrosse becomes the first woman to fly a balloon solo.

SEPTEMBER 16, 1804
Gay-Lussac reaches an altitude of 23,018 feet (7,016 meters) while performing studies of the atmosphere.

1860s
Gaspand-Fèlix Tournachon takes photographs from a balloon in France.

AUGUST 16, 1960
Joe Kittinger breaks the world record for the highest parachute jump from a balloon. He jumps from a height of 102,800 feet (31,333 meters).

MAY 4, 1961
Malcolm Ross and Victor Prather set the world's balloon altitude record of 113,739 feet (34,668 meters).

AUGUST 17, 1978
Maxie Anderson, Ben Abruzzo, and Larry Newman are the first balloon pilots to cross the Atlantic Ocean in *Double Eagle II*.

MAY 12, 1980
Maxie Anderson and his son Kristian complete the first transcontinental flight in *Kitty Hawk*.

NOVEMBER 12, 1981
Rocky Aoki, Ron Clark, Larry Newman, and Ben Abruzzo become the first pilots to fly a balloon across the Pacific Ocean in *Double Eagle V*.

JULY 4, 1987
Per Lindstrand and Richard Branson make the first hot-air balloon flight across the Atlantic Ocean in *Virgin Atlantic Flyer*.

JANUARY 17, 1991
Per Lindstrand and Richard Branson make the first hot-air balloon flight across the Pacific Ocean in *Pacific Flyer*.

MARCH 20, 1999
Bertrand Piccard and Brian Jones complete the first non-stop flight around the world in *Breitling Orbiter 3*.

Chapter 6

The Future of Ballooning

Piccard and Jones completed one of the greatest ballooning accomplishments. But challenges still remain for balloon pilots. They may try to make faster trips around the world or across oceans. They also may attempt to fly for longer periods of time. Some of today's pilots are trying to complete the first solo balloon flight around the world. In 1998, Steve Fossett set the record for the longest distance traveled solo in a balloon. He traveled 14,235 miles (22,908 kilometers). Female pilots may try to become the first woman to complete a flight around the world.

Balloon pilots can set records in many different types of balloons.

Some balloon pilots try to set records by flying cluster balloons.

Setting New Records

Many ballooning experts believe that future pilots will try to break altitude records. They may try to reach altitudes of about 130,000 feet (39,600 meters). The current record is 113,739 feet (34,668 meters). In 1961, Malcolm Ross and Victor Prather set this record in a gas balloon. Per Lindstrand set the current hot-air balloon altitude record. This record is 64,996 feet (19,811 meters).

Some pilots try to set records by using a parachute to jump from a balloon. People use these large pieces of light fabric to float safely to the ground from high places. Joe Kittinger currently holds the world record for the highest parachute jump made from a balloon. On August 16, 1960, he parachuted from a balloon flying at 102,800 feet (31,333 meters).

Other Balloon Types

Balloon pilots who fly long distances use large balloons. These balloons are expensive. Few people can afford them. Most pilots fly small balloons. Some pilots set distance, altitude, and speed records in these balloons.

Some pilots fly cluster balloons. These balloons attach directly to pilots with a harness. They have no gondolas. Cluster balloons are made up of a large group of helium balloons. These balloons can fly at altitudes of about 21,000 feet (6,400 meters).

Balloon pilots continue to meet new challenges and set new records. In the future, balloon pilots may make transoceanic and transcontinental flights in smaller balloons.

Words To Know

envelope (EN-vuh-lope)—a bag made of fabric or plastic that holds gas or hot air in a balloon

gondola (GON-duh-luh)—a basket or enclosed cabin that hangs under a balloon; pilots ride in gondolas.

helium (HEE-lee-uhm)—a lightweight, colorless gas that does not burn

hydrogen (HYE-druh-juhn)—a colorless gas that is lighter than air and catches fire easily

jet stream (JET STREEM)—a strong wind at high altitudes that usually blows from west to east

parachute (PA-ruh-shoot)—a large piece of strong, light fabric; people who jump from high places use parachutes to float safely to the ground.

pilot (PYE-luht)—a person who flies a balloon

To Learn More

Fine, John Christopher. *Free Spirits in the Sky.* New York: Atheneum, 1994.

Keenan, Sheila and Dan Hagedorn, eds. *The Story of Flight: Early Flying Machines, Balloons, Blimps, Gliders, Warplanes, and Jets.* Scholastic Voyages of Discovery. New York: Scholastic, 1995.

Perry, Phyllis J. *Ballooning.* A First Book. New York: Franklin Watts, 1996.

Wallner, Alexandra. *The First Air Voyage in the United States: The Story of Jean-Pierre Blanchard.* New York: Holiday House, 1996.

You can read more about ballooning in *Ballooning: The Journal of the Balloon Federation of America* and *Balloon Life* magazine.

Useful Addresses

Balloon Federation of America
P.O. Box 400
Indianola, IA 50125

Canadian Balloon Association
1610 Alta Vista Drive
Ottawa, ON K1G 0G3
Canada

National Air and Space Museum
Seventh and Independence Avenue SW
Washington, DC 20560

National Geographic Society
1145 17th Street NW
Washington, DC 20036-4688

Internet Sites

BFA Junior Balloonist Page
http://www.bfa-jr-balloonist.com/index.htm

Breitling Orbiter 3
http://www.breitling-orbiter.ch

Canadian Balloon Association
http://www.aeroclub.ca/cba/N2/index.htm

Fédération Aéronautique Internationale (FAI)
http://www.fai.org

National Air and Space Museum
http://www.nasm.edu

Index

Atlantic Ocean, 23, 24, 27, 29, 35, 37

ballast, 9, 12, 25, 31
Breitling Orbiter 3, 5, 36

computers, 13

Double Eagle II, 24–25, 27

envelope, 6, 7, 9, 30, 35

fuel, 12, 19

gondola, 5, 7, 9, 11, 12–13, 20, 24, 30, 43

harness, 43
helium, 9
hydrogen, 8, 9, 19

ice, 23, 24, 30

jet stream, 36, 37
Jules Verne, 35

masks, 13, 24, 30

Pacific Flyer, 32
Pacific Ocean, 29, 30, 32, 35, 36
parachute, 43
photographs, 19–20

Rosie O'Grady, 27

smoke, 15
soldier, 20–21
Solo Challenger, 32
storm, 23, 31

valve, 9
Virgin Atlantic Flyer, 27